Kenzo Amariyo spent nearly four decades learning, practicing and sharing natural medicine and spiritual experiences around various parts of the world bringing much healing into the lives of many others; many of those experiences she shares in her books.

Her personal journey has carried her to Australia, Sedona Arizona, Central America and back to the UK with many vast and varied stops along the way.

Kenzo considers her life an absolute blessing with experiences that have broken her, healed her and woven her into who and what she is today. She holds a PhD. in Natural Medicine, a Post Graduate qualification in Psychology and has vast experience in Shamanic Healing and Counselling.

As a Hermit, she now lives a more quiet life focusing on her childhood desire – writing; she writes poetry and non-fiction.

I dedicate this book to all those who are grieving and all those who are remembering. I hope it brings comfort and inner peace and offers you reconciliation with the idea that:

"Like Birth – Death is Just a Change of Worlds on Our Journey to Enlightenment" – Kenzo

And last but not least, I dedicate this book to my grandson who went before he came. Knowing you existed and still exist is a real blessing; until we meet one day – Nana.

Kenzo Amariyo

POEMS FOR LOVED ONES

In Remembrance of All Those Who Have Returned Home

AUSTIN MACAULEY PUBLISHERS™

LONDON • CAMBRIDGE • NEW YORK • SHARJAH

A CIP catalogue record for this title is available from the British Library.

ISBN 9781528932615 (Paperback)
ISBN 9781528937238 (ePub e-book)

www.austinmacauley.com

First Published 2022
Austin Macauley Publishers Ltd®
1 Canada Square
Canary Wharf
London
E14 5AA

I would like to say:

Thank You to my spouse for always giving me the time I need to think, feel, write and create; without this time my books would never get written.

And:

Thank You to life for all the opportunities to grieve. My losses have enabled me to write this book from a more sincere and compassionate heart.

Poems for Loved Ones has been written for those who are grieving and those who are remembering.

Facing death is never easy, it often brings pain to both those who are dying and those who are left behind.

We all see death differently and our take on death is partly shaped by our upbringing and our views on life. I prefer to see death not as a final curtain but as a stage we must all pass through, like a veil, into something more wonderful. I don't see death as a final chapter but as a journey into a different world.

I believe that we are all spirit beings, having a physical encounter here on earth in a physical body and when our time here is complete, our spirit will need to leave the physical body so it can travel into the next world or next sphere.

Death is never easy, but we can help ourselves by actively choosing to make it a positive experience; we can do this by remembering the positives, remembering the good things that the person did, the good they brought to life, the fun times. We can also help ourselves by actively choosing to forgive what may feel like *the unforgivable*.

We all make mistakes in life, and we can all choose to forgive the mistakes of others. If we all look deep enough, we will find there are also things that we would like to be forgiven for, and no matter how small or big the wrongdoing was, we must, for our own wellbeing, choose forgiveness.

Forgiveness isn't just about the other person, it isn't just about setting the other person free, and it isn't just about whether they deserve the forgiveness, it is about setting ourselves free.

Maybe the person you are crying over or grieving for has hurt you in some way. I ask you today, let it go, forgive them; we all have our story, we are all products of our upbringing, products of society, of life, and we must all find within ourselves the forgiveness necessary for all of our sakes.

Heal your hurts, let go of your anger and ensure you yourself are ready for the next stage of your life. Forgive all those that have hurt you whether they deserve it or not, heal your own hurts or seek help from another to help you heal and be the best you can – just for today.

Flourish and grow into the beautiful person that you truly are – made in the image of the creator, the divine spark, the greater consciousness.

We are all so much more than we realise.

If there is one thing we can all trust, it is the fact that one day we will die. We will die whether we want to or not, whether we are prepared for it or not.

Dying can be traumatic for some and a release for another. One thing is for sure, dying usually leaves much grief in its path. It doesn't seem to matter what we think about dying or where we think we may go, when someone dies, it often causes much heartache and anguish, to say the least.

Some people die unexpectedly and others are aware they are going to die. This chapter is more for those who are aware that their time is drawing nigh; however, this chapter offers suggestions which we can all put into place throughout our lifetime. Feeling that we are ready and prepared for death can sometimes bring inner peace and a sense of relief.

As part of the preparation for dying, we need to take a life review, we need to look back over our life, from as far back as we can remember, scan through the events that come to mind, because they are usually the ones that need looking at.

As you scan through your life, spend time on each moment that occurs, feel the memory, feel the effect it has upon your emotions, your body, your mind. Some of the memories will be happy, others sad. Some will bring up hurt and often unforgiveness.

Forgiveness is a major part of preparing for the forward journey that we are all going to take sooner or later. When people hurt us, we often don't want to forgive; after all, why should we? They hurt us. But in reality, holding onto unforgiveness is like drinking our own poison. Forgiveness can heal two souls, yours and the accused. Sometimes it is hard to forgive, sometimes we feel the hurt is so bad that we can never forgive them, but the truth is, forgiveness is only a choice away. Which sounds really tough for someone who has been abused.

Making the choice to forgive isn't about minimising what has been done or said, it is about realising the healing potential for yourself, as well as the other person. Forgiveness can set you free, it can lift a huge weight off your shoulders, one that you may have been carrying around for years.

One thing I experienced over and over again as a professional counsellor was the relief people felt when they spoke out the words *"I forgive you"* or *"I'm sorry"*. It doesn't mean it is going to be easy and often reaching that point brings many pent-up tears, but the end result is worth every teardrop.

After the life review and dealing with forgiveness, storytelling can be a beautiful healing process, whether it is you telling your own story or whether you are listening to, or encouraging another to tell their own story. We all have good memories no matter how bad our life may have seemed. We all have our own story and yours won't be the same as mine. Yours won't even be the same as your siblings, for we all see life differently and what was okay for one won't be okay for another.

Storytelling isn't about offering or asking for forgiveness; that is behind you, storytelling is about celebrating life, it is about pulling all the beautiful threads of your tapestry of life together and weaving in the ends to create a lasting piece of beauty. You may even want to write it down or record it so those left behind can keep it as your legacy of love.

Another important part of preparing for our journey is remembering to tell people you love them, remembering to utter the final loving words that you want others to remember. Don't wait for this stage, do it whilst you have the opportunity. Our aim is to bless those that have loved us, bless and heal those that have hurt us and free our own souls so that at the right time, our spirit can spread its wings and fly.

So what is death? A good question which we would all answer differently. Our answers would be based on several things, such as what we have been told as children, what our culture, our society has led us to believe about death. Our answer may also involve what our religion or spiritual beliefs have us believe. But one thing with beliefs is that they are fluid. We believe one thing today and tomorrow when we discover something else, we may change how we view the life-death cycle.

Some people believe there is nothing once we die. Some believe in heaven and hell, others believe in a gathering place and no one can tell you that you are right or wrong.

For me personally, I don't believe there is death in the typical sense of it, that being, the body ceases and there is no more. For me, the body will cease just as a flower ceases to live after its time, but I also believe that there is something else, there is something divine, something that started that spark of creation, something so much bigger than ourselves. I do believe that there is a greater consciousness of which we are all part and parcel of, that we are all tiny drops of one grand divine ocean.

I believe:

"Like birth, death is just a change of worlds on our journey to enlightenment."

Just a change of worlds. If we could hang onto that, it has the potential to bring so much release, it has the potential to truly ease the concerns of departure.

I believe that we are spirit beings having a human experience here on earth. When our experience is over, we will need to leave our body one way or another, we will need to drop our robes in order for us to return home, home to the spiritual realm. Back to where we came from, we will perhaps be absorbed into universal energy. No one really knows.

Some people claim to have had near-death experiences of which we have no right to discredit, some of those experiences have taken people to what they believe to be the after-life.

There are many ideas in religion and spiritual circles about the after-life. It doesn't matter whether you believe you will be sitting at the feet of Jesus, singing to God, being absorbed into a Greater Consciousness, and it doesn't matter whether you believe in spheres and the ability or necessity to work through such spheres until you reach enlightenment.

What really matters is that you know what you believe in and can hang onto that and feel secure with it. What really matters is that you feel good within yourself and ready to meet whatever the next journey through life holds for you. And who knows, that may be different for you and me.

At the end of the day, I believe we all walk the same circle of life, we just stand on different spokes of the wheel and where one is today, I could be tomorrow. I believe that each spiritual spoke will eventually, through love and compassion, bring all back to the centre, the centre of existence, whatever you want to call *'It'*.

At the end of the day, life and death are about love and compassion, for others and for ourselves. We fulfil our lives not by how much money we have, who we knew, what job we had, but by the amount of souls that we touched whilst here on the earth.

Love and compassion are what will carry us safely home.

Oh… how we wish we could skip this part, we can often manage the dying, reasonably accept the death on a physical level, but oh… how we hate the grief.

We hate the grief that rips our heart apart, that causes the tsunami of emotions – anger, tears, loss, and at times blame, that can overwhelm us and leave us feeling ravished as by a tidal wave or hurricane. We hate the very thing that in time will bring us relief, acceptance and a certain amount of peace. We hate the very thing that will in time bring healing.

It is inevitable that loss brings pain and heartache no matter how religious or spiritual we are and this sense of pain and loss doesn't just happen to humans, animals can and often do grieve for their losses too. Which means we were made to feel pain, not just happiness; we were made to feel sadness, not just joy, we were made to feel both ends of the spectrum in order to help us to be and feel whole in our experiences through life.

The cycle of grief has different stages, many say there are five stages which we all go through, which are: denial, anger, bargaining, depression and acceptance.

However, these stages are not pit stops, we don't go through denial and then move onto anger; the stages of grief are fluid. We will pass through them and return to them often many times before we can reach a permanent place of acceptance.

When acceptance calls, it can be a real blessing, but it can often bring feelings of guilt. Some people feel guilty for moving on, for accepting the death, some feel like they are letting the deceased down, these are all issues that need dealing with, and some will need a counsellor to help them get through them.

Acceptance is a beautiful place to arrive at because it means you are ready to move on. Moving on doesn't necessarily mean location or in love, it can just mean you are at peace with your loss and you are ready to start rebuilding what has felt like shattered glass. A seed of hope is now starting to grow within, you are starting to accept your new life, life without your loved one, or at least accept that your life does and will and often must go on during and after your loss.

Family and friends need to be a support for you, you may even want to join a support group with others who really do know how you feel. Some may need help from the doctor, others from work colleagues. We all have different needs and we need to feel brave enough to ask for the help we need. It takes a strong person to ask for help and an even stronger one to actually accept it.

Never feel ashamed if you need help, never feel as if you are a let-down because it has been months and you still aren't *over it*. We all heal in our own time and we must respect ourselves enough to give ourselves enough space to be able to heal.

At first you may use distraction and keep yourself so busy that you don't have time to process the loss. This is fine for a short time, but over time, you will need to make time to grieve, you will need to make time to go through the cycle of grief, because if you don't, the day will come when things will sneak up on you and out of the blue, for seemingly no reason at all, you will have a psychological or emotional breakdown.

We must look after ourselves and not tell ourselves to snap out of it. Find what helps you heal and use those healthy tools. Resist the temptation to turn to alcohol or drugs, or other unhealthy coping mechanisms.

Remember, the cycle of grief is your freedom, not your bondage.

Time has passed, you have cried enough tears to fill a dam, you've been angry, sad and all else that comes with grief, but suddenly, you find yourself on the other side.

You are finally ready to move on.

Moving on doesn't mean you are going to forget the person. You may have made up new memoirs filled with photos or poems or even cards from that person, some people make a small shrine in their home in memory of that special one. We all remember differently and that is what moving on is about. It is the recognition that the person is *gone but not forgotten* and for many that is really important.

Moving on doesn't mean you won't still cry sometimes, you may find a specific song or memory brings back the tears; let them flow, don't push them down, they need to come out and be expressed. Think of these times as the aftershock of an earthquake, there is usually a rumble still left to come, see it as the final cleaning-up of the little bits and pieces of glass that were scattered on the floor when life fell and broke.

Moving on may mean that it's time to make new plans, new decisions. For some that means moving home; for others it means clearing out the belongings of the dear one. It means different things for different people and you must find what it means for you and honour it.

Moving on is like starting life over, it is an opportunity to create something new, an opportunity to weave different threads into a fresh tapestry of life and love.

If you are reading this, I truly hope and pray that the following poems are a blessing to you and your family throughout your journey or their journey. Poetry can be a beautiful healing tool, it can stir emotions and bring a sense of peace.

I hope your journey through life is filled with much love and compassion and I urge you to be the change you want to see in the world. Love and forgive always, for we never truly know what is around the corner. Treat people with courtesy even when they are rude, I always tell myself:

"You never know what is going on in their life, someone close may have just died."

Treat yourself well, nurture yourself physically, emotionally and spiritually.

And finally…

Always Walk in Peace.

The time has come
To say goodbye
It's time to stretch
My wings and fly.

I haven't left you
All alone
But now have freedom
So I can roam.

Through space, past stars
The moon to rest
Feel me resting
Upon your chest.

I'm the little bird
The floating feather
Always here
Whatever the weather.

So close your eyes
And open your heart
Feel me within
For we'll never part.

Love can move mountains
Love can heal pain.
Today you are grieving
Tomorrow the same.

But a day will come
When your tears cease to fall.
That is the day
When acceptance calls.

Your life will go on
Like a growing tree.
You'll put out new branches
You'll let go of me.

I will always be here
Just look to your heart.
And there you will find me
For we'll never part.

How my heart aches
Like a broken wing.
What I would give
Just to hear you sing.

Not just a melody
Not just a song.
But a chorus of love
To make me feel strong.

If I could just hear
Your voice one more time
I'd know in my heart
You'll always be mine.

The sounds of your chatter
Your laughter, your smile.
You lit up my life
For a very long while.

You touched me so deeply
You pulled at my heart.
And now you're not here
Life's fallen apart.

But for you I will live
Forever and a day.
Until once again
We meet, come what may.

I'll not lose my hope
Nor end my new life
For I know you are watching
My beloved, my wife.

No more suffering
And no more pain.
I know your life
Won't be the same.

But, honey, please
Remember this.
I finally have
My heartfelt wish.

I now can truly
Start to fly.
No more heartache
I no longer cry.

I feel the wind
Beneath my wings.
My Spirit is free
And my Soul doth sing.

Sing from your hearts
Rejoice for my death.
It is only a passing
A final breath.

Like the bird when it leaps
From the tree's highest branch.
It spreads its wings
It starts to dance.

As it rides the wind
And soars the sky
It doesn't ask how
It doesn't ask why.

It simply trusts
In what it can't see.
The miracle of life
Of life's mystery.

The trumpet is blowing
The Angels rejoice.
My presence is needed
My Spirit, my voice.

The Angels are coming
Their songs fill my ear.
This is my time
Don't mourn love, just cheer.

My purpose is done
My day has drawn nigh.
It now is my turn
To go home – don't cry.

The arms of Great Mystery
Are waiting for me.
Love and tranquillity
I send to thee.

It's raining here
There is no light.
My life just seems
Like one long night.

My love has gone
She's far away.
She's spread her wings
Just another day.

Her sun has risen
Pain no more.
Is it now my turn?
Where is the door?

The door that brings
Welcome relief
From all the suffering
All the grief.

The veil has lifted
The trumpets sound.
My dearly loved one
Won't be around.

I'll awake and look
But see her not.
Yet all the memories
I'll not have forgot.

That first sweet kiss
That tender hold.
The fun, the laughter
She was so bold.

My first true love
She's gone away
To a place of peace
Where we'll meet one day.

I never saw her laugh or cry
She was never happy
I don't know why.

She had all things
Most people dream
A house, car, yacht
It would make you beam.

Yet all I saw
Was sorrow and pain.
A life that seemed wasted
An emotional drain.

Maybe now
She'll find some peace
And a life filled with treasures
My sweet little niece.

Oh, for the time
When we meet once again.
Singing and dancing
My dear, dear friend.

Oh, how we laughed
And at times didn't we cry.
Now we are separated
Why, oh, why?

You were such a rare gift
On a dreary day.
I always felt love
Coming from your way.

You were such an Angel
While here on earth.
Now you are gone
Ready for rebirth.

You were the rose in my life
The scent in the air.
Oh, for you
How much I did care.

Our life was filled
With laughter and love.
A precious gift
That came from above.

And now you are gone
So far away.
The pain is immense
But what I will say IS

I will never forget you
Not even one day.
For our love and devotion
Is here to stay.

Don't cry, my love
Can you not feel me near?
Come a little closer
I'll kiss away your tear.

You look so broken
But your heart will mend.
Just give it time
My love I do send.

I won't forget you
I won't go away.
I'm here if you need me
Just call out and pray.

I'll touch your face
I'll kiss your cheek.
I'll carry you always
Whenever you're weak.

Don't cry, my love
For it breaks my heart.
I will always be with you
We will never part.

Thank you for the time we had
For all the good and all the bad.

The good gave us strength
The bad made us grow.

You're the best thing that happened
In my life – did you know?

I have no regrets, just great memories
I'll never forget you, in you I believe.

You were always my heaven, my stars and my earth
Your weight in gold you were truly worth.

I daily give thanks to God from above
For my sweet precious husband, now in the arms of love.

You stole my heart, or did I give it away?
I will always love you, forever and a day.

My heart is broken in two
You're gone and there's nothing I can do.
My tears flow like a pouring rain
Every drop carries a full load of pain.

My heart is broken in two
My life has ended with you.
No more laughter and love, just pain
How I wish you were here once again.

My heart is broken in two
I can't survive without you.
You were the beat of my heart, the song on my breath.
And now you're gone, taken by death.

My heart is broken in two.

Don't leave me crying
With a broken heart.
Don't go just yet
Don't let us part.

You're my world, my love
My everything.
I hold you close
You make my heart sing.

Don't leave me crying
Filled with fear
Wishing my loved one
Was still really near.

Don't leave me crying
In a world of no hope.
I can't face the future
I can't seem to cope.

Don't leave me crying
I've not said goodbye.
Just stay for a moment
I don't want you to die.

I can see the light
They are coming for you.
My world, my love – gone
Whatever will I do?

Love will save the day
My love has gone away.
But memories fill my heart
So I know we won't really part.

The pain is very deep
For my sweetheart has gone to sleep.
But memories fill my heart
So I know we won't really part.

Although I'm broken in two
I'll never stop loving you.
Love will save the day
My love has gone away.

Fear not, my love
'Tis not the end.
I feel you near
My love I doth send.

I feel your touch
Your whisper in my ear.
These are the things
I will hold so dear.

Fear not, my love
'Tis not the end.
I feel your love
And my love I doth send.

It's not what we wanted
But at least you are near.
My sweetheart, my love
Whom I cherish so dear.

I hear His voice calling me
I know He wants me home.
I'm torn between two loves
In two worlds I wish to roam.

My years have been too short
I thought I had much time.
But seems no longer possible
To hold this love of mine.

I hear His voice calling me
No longer will He wait.
The Angels have arrived
To carry me to the gate.

My love will never falter
My love won't dissipate.
But heal and move on swiftly
Don't close love's door – don't wait.

You were my life
You were everything.
Our love reflected
In our wedding ring.

Our life was filled
With laughter and tears.
We shared so much
Throughout the years.

Ups and downs
Happiness and sorrow.
We had enough love
To face tomorrow.

Now we are here
Death do us part.
Yet life will go on
It's a brand-new start.

Time will heal
And I must go on.
Until we meet again
My beloved one.

Two peas in a pod
We were so much the same.
Now you have gone
I feel so much pain.

The pod seems so empty
Without you there.
I'll never stop loving you
I will always care.

Love is forever
No matter how blue.
Ups and downs
But I still love you.

You were my strength
Hope in times of need.
You were part of my dreams
That tiny seed.

You watered my hopes
You wiped away tears.
So much love
In so many years.

It now seems unfair
As you're ready to fly.
One last trip
I can't help but cry.

But life will go on
Forever and a day.

Until once again
We meet up and say...

Love is forever.

I hear your tears in the raindrops
Your laughter in the brook.
I see your smile in the sunshine
Your heartfelt song in the rook.

I no longer see your body
But I know you are around.
I see you in all of nature
In every sweet, sweet sound.

Your presence in the wind
Your touch from the breeze.
I rest assured you're here
I can now sleep with ease.

You're the first sign of spring
The summer and my dreams.
You hold me gently still
So my face lights up and beams.

I cook your favourite dish
I wear your favourite shirt.
I drink from your favourite glass
But oh, how my heart does hurt.

I watch your favourite show
Sleep at your side of the bed.
But no matter what I do
I can't get you from my head.

I play your favourite songs
Sit in your window seat.
But no matter what
My heart is missing a beat.

The beat I always felt
Whenever you were around.
The beat that kept me living
And held me safe and sound.

Blue skies overhead
Remind me of you.
Sunshine and laughter
In all that you do.

Nothing was trouble
Nothing to regret.
You just loved your life
I'm so glad that we met.

Years of much joy
Years of much love.
But now you are gone
You are far, far above.

Above all the mountains
And into the sky.
Life seems unfair
I keep asking, *why*?

You brought so much happiness
To those you embraced.
You lit up their lives
With your sweet, happy face.

Now you are gone
An empty world behind.
My special Angel
A one of a kind.

Fly, little one
Fly really high.
Don't look back
Don't even sigh.

One minute you're here
The next you were gone.
One minute a blessing
Now just a song.

A song in my heart
A sweet memory.
We'll meet once again
It'll be real Heavenly.

Love me tender
Don't hold too tight.
When it's time to go
I'll follow the light.

Like a dove in your hand
That needs to fly free.
Love but let go
Don't hold tight to me.

We all have our time
When Heaven calls us home.
It isn't a bad place
But a place to roam.

We can stretch our wings
We can finally fly free.
If you go first
Please wait for me.

Never apart
Always together.
I will love you, honey
Forever and ever.

Kiss me, honey
Kiss my lips.
Let me taste you one more time.

Kiss me, honey
Kiss my lips.
Let me feel that you are mine.

Kiss me, honey
Kiss my tears.
I can feel I'm slipping away.

Kiss me, honey,
Kiss me goodbye.
We'll meet again one day.

Blue skies are above
But clouds do fill my heart.
I truly thought
We would never part.

I never believed
"*Until death do us part.*"
I somehow thought
You'd always fill my heart.

I thought life would give
An eternity with you.
I somehow feel cheated
Down and blue.

The skies may be blue
The sun may shine brightly.
But you have now gone
You've gone to the Almighty.

And I'm left in tatters
I don't want this new life.
I'm now all alone
I just want my wife.

I want what we had
You were my life and my soul.
And now you're gone
Leaving a gaping hole.

Blue skies are above
But clouds do fill my heart.
I truly thought
We would never part.

Incessant chatter fills my head
I can't believe you are now dead.
I thought that time was on our side
I thought we still had time to ride.

Time to ride the waves of life
Time to be with my dear wife.
Time to laugh and time to love
What was He thinking from above?

Incessant chatter fills my head
Thoughts keep coming now you're dead.
All I think both day and night.
Is… *Should have done this, should have got this right.*

Now I am left with grief and sorrow
Grieving today, regretting tomorrow.
For tomorrow is now void of my love
Taken so swiftly from the arms of love.

Forgive now
Before it's too late.
You never know
When Heaven's gate

Is going to open
And call back home
The love of your life
To freely roam.

Unforgiveness
Hurts more than one soul.
It acts like a poison
It won't make you whole.

It takes away life
It suffocates love.
It stops the blessings
From above.

Love is the answer
Love is the way.
We all need forgiveness
Day after day.

No one is perfect
No one's so pure.
That they don't need forgiveness
And God's love for sure.

So wait no longer
Take that big breath.
Say *"I forgive you"*
Let God do the rest.

Then wait and see
How love starts to flow.
In both of your hearts
And then you will know.

That love heals all hurts
No matter how deep.
It clears the way
For good memories to keep.

It clears the head
Releases hearts.
Then you can rest
Knowing love won't depart.

On a beautiful day
With sun shining bright
A man said *"Hello"*
Which caused a bright light

To catch my attention
I was struck in the heart.
I knew from then
We would never part.

We've been through valleys
And scaled many mountains.
We've laughed and we've cried
And buried a fountain.

A fountain of hurt
Of deep pain and tears.
The things that we've felt
Over the years.

But no matter what
Life has dished out.
We have stayed together
Sorted life out.

And here we are
At the end of the trail.
And all we can hear
Is God's mighty hail.

Saying, *"Well done*
You made it at last.
And your love for each other
Remains deep and vast.

"For nothing can break
What I bring together.
When true love meets
It lasts forever."

Mothers are Angels
That gave up their wings.
They make our life good
With so many things.

They give up their body
To carry, endure pain.
They give of themselves
Their work is our gain.

They hold us, they scold us
They keep us in line.
They give us the freedom
We want when it's time.

They turn bread and water
To mouth-watering feasts.
But boy, don't cross them
The tongue of a beast.

They'll lash you with words
You'll turn pale from their looks.
Don't run away
You'll be caught by the crook.

Better you just love them
And thank them for all.
They all do their best
Though many do fall.

They fall from great heights
Some feel so let down.
But we have to remember
They too wear a crown.

For no one is perfect
And each gives their all.
We have to remember
Their life's not a ball.

They too carry pain
And hurts in their heart.
A continuous cycle
Right from the start.

But nonetheless
Remember just this.
Because of these Angels
Life is more bliss.

So if death is awaiting
And darkness draws nigh
Make sure you forgive
Or you'll regret it and cry.

Remember the good things
Forget all the rest.
And say, *"Mum, you're an Angel*
You're truly the best.

"If time could go back
And I chose my own mum
It would still be you
For all that you've done."

Fathers are Saints
Despite what we think.
Some are real softies
Hiding tears with a blink.

They may hold their feelings
Close to their heart.
But they always love us
Right from the start.

They try to guide us
To all things good.
They work finger to bone
They'd give you their blood.

They love you, they hold you
They watch your back.
And if you're a girl
Future boys will get flack.

They'll be watched like a hawk
Going in for its prey.
One wrong foot
And they're dead, right away.

Fathers are Saints
Even though halo's slip.
And words can come out
That feel like a whip.

But under it all
Is a warm, squidgy dad
Who has lots of charm
And often acts mad.

But humour quite often
Goes a long way.
When times are tough
It can save the day.

His heart is big
And his love is endearing.
He'll empty his pockets
To buy you those earrings.

He'll sneak things out
Saying, *"Don't tell your mum*
She'll kill me tomorrow
So don't be so dumb.

"You get me in trouble
I'll cover you no more.
I'll tell her the stories
And she'll drop to the floor."

So fathers are not
Just Saints, don't you see.
You can easily bend them
A tool they can be

To get what you want
From Mum and from life
That's why it's good
If your dad has a wife.

When one says no
The other will say yes.
Just keep on milking it
It's really the best.

So forgive all the wrongs
Let Dad off the hook.
He's your dad and a loving
Saint from a book.

Family is family
It's just what it is.
Fathers and mothers
It's not always bliss.

Brothers and sisters
Fighting all day.
Sometimes wishing
They'd all go away.

But now death has come
And all things stand still.
Time seems to freeze
Tears flow at will.

Suddenly, fights
And disputes seem so small.
Suddenly, grief
Makes you all fall.

As you drop to your knees
Sorry for things said
You now can see
You were just a hothead.

But now they are gone
Forever and a day.
So you need to make peace
With yourself anyway.

Speak words of forgiveness
Love and hope.
Hang onto the good times
It will help you cope.

Don't live in fear
Hate or regret.
Always be thankful
That you all met.

We never know when
Our time has drawn nigh.
Don't waste life fighting
You'll regret it and cry.

Fill up your life
With laughter and cheer.
Let go of hurts
They don't serve you, my dear.

Only love
Can fill in the gap
Where family hurt you
When it felt like a slap.

Only forgiveness
Can heal you today.
So reach out and forgive
Come what may.

The time has come
To say farewell.
Some think of heaven
Some think of hell.

I choose to believe
In a field of fresh roses
Where weeping willows
Bend in sweet poses.

I like to think
It's a journey of life
With no more sorrow
No more strife.

Death is not death
But heaven's door
Where I will live
My life once more.

Daddy went to heaven today
My happiness has gone away.
Who'll tie my shoes and ruff my hair?
Who'll carry me up the winding stair?

How could God take him from our home?
Now we're all sad and all alone.
I know God needed another Saint
But it's not okay, it really ain't.

Mummy's crying, her voice is low
I heard her asking God, *"Why so?"*
I know she's hurting really bad
Now we're all feeling very sad.

But Mummy said, *"He's in the sky
Shining brightly and that's why
Because God needed one more light
To make the night sky much more bright."*

Mummy went away today
She spread her wings, so Daddy says.
She flew real high into the sky
She went so quickly, I don't know why.

Now Daddy's crying many tears
I hear him talking about the years.
The years they had with so much love
But now she's gone far up above.

I think because she's gone so far
That she will turn into a star
And light the way for many more
So they can find heaven's door.

Daddy's crying in the chair
He looks a mess, not brushed his hair.
I know he's missing Mummy too
But I don't know what I must do.

I ask him, *"Daddy, you okay?"*
He wipes his tears and then he says:
"I am, my little angel dear
Fear not, you know your daddy's here.

"All is well because you're here
Sent from God to ease my fear.
It's you and me now, we'll never part
Because you hold me in your heart.

"Mummy went back home to love
God the Father from above."

Mummy said she's going away
And I can't go, that I must stay.

I must stay to hold Dad's heart
So that it doesn't tear apart.

I must hold him tight each night
And fall asleep till day breaks light.

Mummy said I'm going to die
Must not worry, for I will fly
Far past the stars to heaven's gate
Where God with arms outstretched will wait.

He'll hold me close and hold me tight
He'll tuck me into bed at night.
He'll feed me well and make me laugh
He'll wipe my tears whilst in the bath.

Mummy said heaven's just like here
And God will keep me year on year.
She said dear Granny went in May
So maybe with her I can stay.

My baby's going home today
To rest with God every day.
Tubes come out, machines turned off
No more pain, no more cough.

The only pain is in my heart
Can't bear the thought we'll be apart.
All I can do is trust one day
In my arms you will lay.

Go tomorrow, not today
Just stay a little while.
Go tomorrow, not today
For I'll miss your loving smile.

Go tomorrow, not today
I'm not ready to let you go.
Go tomorrow, not today
Then to heaven you can say, *"Hello."*

My grandson went
Before he came.
Life will never
Be the same.

Three years on
And still crying.
And about that
I'm not lying.

You never expect
To bury your offspring
And certainly not
Your offspring's offspring.

A little white coffin
Took him away
To the arms of love
Where we'll meet one day.

Never an answer
Not knowing why
Makes you ask
Why do babies die?

Watch over me from far above
Keep me safe, send me love.
Let me know you're still around
Don't forget me, send a sound.

A sound of birds in the air
To tell me once again you care.
A ripple in the babbling brook
A hidden message in a book.

Send your love upon a breeze
A little tickle to make me sneeze.
Do the things I love the most
My precious sweetheart, my lover's Ghost.

Be not afraid, the time will come
We'll leave this earth, God's will be done.
We'll fly the skies and not be bound
We'll chase the rainbow, not make a sound.

Those left will shed their heartfelt tears
They'll remember love from all those years.
But yesterday has gone – no more
For God has now opened the door.

We're free to go where we desire
Nothing to hold us, I admire.
Here and there and everywhere
Finally free without a care.

Shine a light so I can see
Shine it brightly over me.
Shine it always, day and night
Like the sun, warm and bright.

Stand close by, still touch my face
Till one day we find that place
Where both of us can reunite
And soar like eagles to greater heights.

If I could paint a picture
I'd paint it just of you.
I'd use so many colours
With every type of hue.

I'd paint it like a rainbow
I'd paint it big and bright.
I'd hang it in each room
To remind me of your light.

You gave me so much hope, dear
You gave me so much love.
But now you're gone away
On a journey far above.

I'll wait for that one day
When we will meet again.
Although I don't know how
Then there'll be no pain.

But all I can now do
Is wait till such a time
When once again, my sweetie
I'll be yours and you'll be mine.

I see a bright, bright light
Brightly shining as the sun.
I feel my spirit lifting
I know this day is done.

I float past roofs and tree tops
Whilst only looking straight.
I float past clouds and stars
Heading for Heaven's gate.

I'm met with love, compassion
Forgiveness fills my heart.
A brand-new life beckons me
It's a brand-new start.

If you've reached the end
Of this small book of prose
You'll now understand
Just how life goes.

The birth-life-death cycle
Happens to all.
You'll go when it's time
Or not at all.

I hope this brought comfort
And eased some deep pain.
I wish you well
Till we meet once again.